A New True Book

INSECTS

By Illa Podendorf

This "true book" was prepared
under the direction of
Illa Podendorf,
formerly with the Laboratory School,
University of Chicago

CHILDRENS PRESS, CHICAGO

Ten-lined June Beetle

PHOTO CREDITS

Charles L. Hogue, Ph. D.—2, 4, 7 (right), 9 (left, bottom), 10 (middle), 20 (2 photos), 21, 25, 31, 35 (bottom left), 36 (3 photos)

Lynn M. Stone—6, 9 (left, top and above right), 13 (right), 15 (2 photos), 19 (bottom left and right), 27 (bottom), 35 (top left), 40, 41 (2 photos), 43 (left), 44 (3 photos).

Jerry Hennen—10 (bottom), 17 (bottom), 22 (bottom), 38, 43 (right)

James P. Rowan—Cover, 7 (left), 10 (top), 13 (left), 19 (top), 22 (top), 35 (right), 45

United States Department of Agriculture: USDA—12, 17 (top), 27 (top), 29, 33

Cover—grasshopper

Library of Congress Cataloging in Publication Data

Podendorf, Illa.
   Insects.
   (A New true book)
   Previously published as: The true book of insects. 1954.
   Summary: Briefly introduces some distinctive characteristics, habits, similarities, and differences of a number of different insects.
   1. Insects—Juvenile literature. [1. Insects] I. Title.
QL467.2.P62   1981   595.7   81-7689
ISBN 0-516-01627-X   AACR2

36832 BTSB ⁴/93

TABLE OF CONTENTS

Green Fruit Beetle

INSECTS ARE ANIMALS

Insects are animals.
Animals need food.
Animals need air.
Animals grow and help make animals just like themselves.
Most animals can move about.

Hummingbird Moth on Swamp Milkweed

Insects eat many kinds of food.

Hummingbird Moths are insects. They get their food from flowers.

Giant Water Bug

Common Ground Beetle

Some insects live in water.

Some insects live in the ground.

Other insects live on leaves or in trees.

Wherever insects live, they are able to get air.

Almost all insects lay eggs. Insects lay eggs in many kinds of places.

One mother cricket lays her eggs in the ground.

Other kinds of crickets lay eggs in plant stems.

Top left: **Cecropia Moth laying egg cluster**
Left: Giant Silk Moth
Above: Treehopper

Insects move about in many ways.

Moths have wings and fly. Most moths fly at night.

Other insects crawl on the ground.

Longhorn Beetle

Ladybird Beetle

Imperial Moth

INSECTS ARE ALIKE IN SOME WAYS

Almost all grown-up insects have six legs. The six legs of an Imperial Moth are hard to see.

Grasshopper

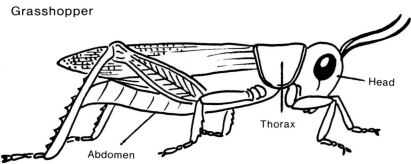

Insects have three body parts.

The body parts of a grasshopper are easy to see.

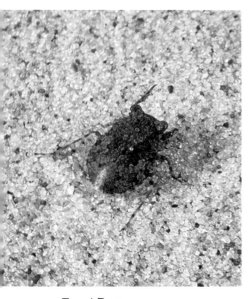

Toad Bug

Red Admiral

The body parts of a
Toad Bug are hard to see.
Most insects have wings.
Butterflies have four
wings. Most butterflies fly
in the daytime.

INSECTS CHANGE AS THEY GROW UP

A mother butterfly lays eggs. The eggs hatch into caterpillars. Each caterpillar makes a case, called a chrysalis, about itself. A grown-up butterfly comes from the chrysalis.

Cecropia Moths change, too. The case the Cecropia Moth makes is called a cocoon. The cocoon is made of silk.

Cecropia Moth

Cecropia Moth, cocoon

Cecropia Moth, caterpillar

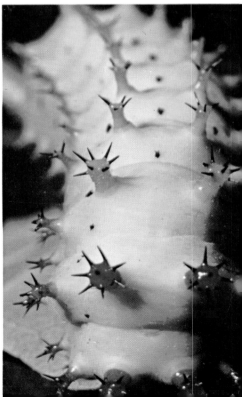

Mosquitoes change as they grow up. They live in water part of their lives.

Only grown-up mosquitoes can fly.

Other insects live in the ground part of their lives.

Mosquito

Mosquito larva or wiggler

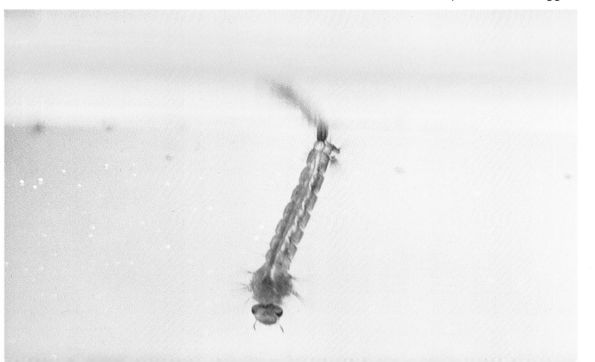

The Monarch Butterfly caterpillar makes a green and gold case. It is called a chrysalis.

This caterpillar eats milkweed.

Monarch larva

Monarch chrysalis

Monarch Butterfly leaving chrysalis

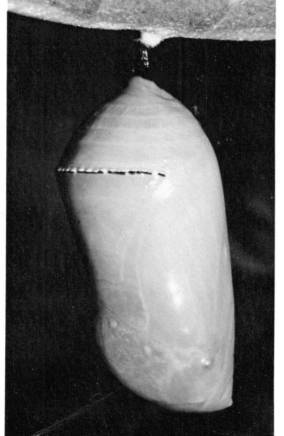

Left: White-lined Sphinx caterpillar
Above: White-lined Sphinx Moth

There are different kinds
of Sphinx Moths.

One kind lays eggs on
tomato plants. Its caterpillar
eats the plants. Then the
caterpillar makes its case
in the ground.

Painted Tiger Moth

The Tiger Moth caterpillar eats the leaves of shade trees. It does its growing while it is a caterpillar.

Guess what the Cabbage Butterfly caterpillar eats. CABBAGE!

Young Grasshopper

Praying Mantis

A mother grasshopper lays many eggs. Tiny grasshoppers hatch from the eggs. These tiny grasshoppers grow to be big grasshoppers.

A Praying Mantis lives among plants. It is hard to see when it is on a plant. Its young hatch from eggs in spring.

SOME INSECTS LIVE ALONE

Wasps that live alone are called solitary wasps. A Mud Dauber Wasp is a solitary wasp.

Click Beetles live alone.

When a Click Beetle is on its back, it flips itself into the air and lands right side up. As it flips itself over, it makes a clicking sound.

Yellow-and-Black Mud Dauber Wasp

SOME INSECTS LIVE IN LARGE FAMILIES

Honeybees make homes in hollow trees. Sometimes they make a box a home. This box is called a bee-hive. The place where hives are kept is called an apiary.

Beekeeper with Honeybees

Honeybee nest

Mother bees are queens. There is usually only one queen in each hive.

Father bees are called drones. There are only a few drones in each hive.

But each hive has many more workers than either drones or queens.

Each bee has its own work to do.

Bees in hive

Some bees make honey.
Some bees clean the
hive.

Some bees feed the
queen.

Some bees guard the
hive.

Red Mound Ant

Ants live in large families.

There are many kinds of ants. Some ants live in trees. Black Ants live in the ground. Some ants even try to live in our houses!

The ant queen lays all the eggs. Each egg hatches into a tiny larva. The larva makes a cocoon about itself.

More queens, more males, and many, many workers hatch from the cocoons.

California Harvester Ant

Soon the new queens and males leave to make homes of their own.

Each ant worker does its own kind of work.

Some ants are nurses.

Some ants hunt food.

Some ants clean the home.

Some ants are soldiers.

Carpenter Ants

Ants do interesting things.

Some ants milk plant-lice like farmers milk cows.

Some ants carry leaves like parasols.

Carpenter Ants cut wood.

SOME INSECTS ARE FINE BUILDERS

Termites are not ants. They build their homes in wood. They eat the wood as they build their homes.

Paper Wasps build their homes with paper. They make their own paper.

Mud Daubers make their homes of mud.

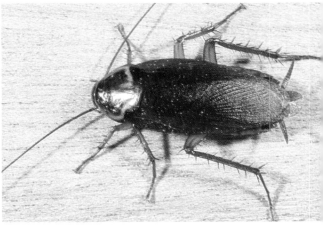

Top left: Hornet Nest
Left: Golden Paper Wasp
Above: American Cockroach

SOME INSECTS ARE
FAST RUNNERS

Cockroaches are very fast runners. It is hard to catch them. They run and hide very fast.

Domestic Silk Moth, larva

Domestic Silk Moth, cocoon   Domestic Silk Moth, female

SOME INSECTS ARE FINE SPINNERS

Silkworms are the very best spinners. They spin silk for their cocoons.

People use the silk they spin. Silkworms are raised for their silk.

Silkworms eat mulberry leaves.

Polyphemus Moth

Polyphemus Moths spin silk for their cocoons. It is not as fine as the silk that the silkworms make.

Luna Moths spin a thread for their cocoons, too.

SOME INSECTS ARE FAST FLIERS

Dragonflies are very fast fliers.

Dragonfly

Painted Lady

Sulphur Butterfly

Butterflies like these are
good fliers, too.

MORE INTERESTING INSECTS

It is an interesting fact that Lightning Bugs have their own lights. Have you ever seen a Lightning Bug?

There are thousands of kinds of flies. All flies have two wings.

Flies are about the fastest flying insects. A fly can move its wings 200 times in just one second. When its wings move this fast you can hear a buzzing sound.

Robber Fly on Blazing Star   Migrating Monarch Butterflies

Many Monarch Butterflies get together and fly south for the winter. Not many other kinds of insects do this.

Insects protect themselves in interesting ways.

Top left: Monarch Butterfly
Left: Viceroy Butterfly
Above: Walking Stick

Birds do not often eat these Viceroy Butterflies because they look so much like Monarch Butterflies. Birds seem to know Monarch Butterflies have a bad taste.

When a Walking Stick sits very still on a twig, it looks like a twig. It is hard for an enemy to find it.

A Katydid is green. Its wings look like green leaves.

Insects are very interesting. They are fun to watch as they work.

Katydid

WORDS YOU SHOULD KNOW

apiary(AY • pee • air • ee) — a place where bees are kept

case(KAYSS) — a container

caterpillar(KAT • er • pill • er) — a moth or butterfly after it has hatched from an egg

cocoon(kuh • KOON) — a case made by a caterpillar and in which it develops

chrysalis(KRISS • uh • liss) — a case made by a caterpillar and spun around it

crawl — to move slowly

drone — a male bee

enemy(EN • ih • mee) — not a friend

guard(GARD) — to keep safe; protect

hatch(HACH) — to come out of the egg

hive(HYVE) — a home for bees

hollow(HOLL • oh) — having an empty space inside

insect(IN • sekt) — a small animal with six legs and three body parts

interesting(IN • ter • es • ting) — to hold attention

larva(LAR • vuh) — an insect which has just hatched from an egg

male — being a man

parasol(PAIR • uh • soll) — a small umbrella used to protect a person from the sun

plant lice — an insect that lives on plants

protect(proh • TEKT) — to keep safe; free from harm; guard

milk — to press out a liquid

raise(RAYZ) — to bring up and take care of

solitary(SOL • ih • tair • ee) — living alone; be by oneself

spin — to form a thread from a liquid given off by the body

stem — main supporting part of a plant

thread(THRED) — a fine thin strand of fiber

tiny — very very small

trap — something for catching animals

twig — a small branch of a tree or shrub

INDEX

About the Author

Born and raised in western Iowa, Illa has had experience teaching science at both elementary and high school levels. For many years she served as head of Science Dept., Laboratory School, University of Chicago and is currently consultant on the series of True Books and author of many of them. A pioneer in creative teaching, she has been especially successful in working with the gifted child.